THE CROW AND THE SHEEP

There was once a naughty crow. She was very proud of herself.

She felt that the animals and birds should all obey her.

She also liked to trouble others. One day, the crow was very bored.

She flew into a meadow where she saw many sheep.

The crow flew over to a sheep and seated herself on the sheep's back.

The crow said, "I am tired of flying. Will you carry me around?"

The sheep was timid and rarely said no to anyone.

So, she carried the crow around wherever she went.

She could not graze for long, as the crow's claws poked her back.

Soon, she was tired. She said, "If you had treated a dog this way, he would have bitten you with his sharp teeth!"

The crow said in annoyance, "Do I look like a fool to you?"

"I only order around those who are weak and cannot refuse," she added.

The crow knew exactly whom to bully and whom to flatter.

The cunning and the selfish should not be feared.

Keywords

naughty   trouble
tired   timid
poked   annoyance